Dave Lewis is from Cilfynydd, always lived in Wales except fc spent far too many years as a at numerous other profession:

He has written sports articles for the BBC and columns for local newspapers and web sites. He continues to run several web sites including the popular Pontypridd Town Online.

He is founder and organiser of The Welsh Poetry Competition, an international competition which seeks to encourage and nurture talented writers that have been overlooked by the arts establishment in Wales.

This collection of poetry stretches from 1985-2009. For more information visit Dave's web site.

www.david-lewis.co.uk

Dave Lewis

Layer Cake

A collection of poetry from 1985-2009

Published by:
Ponty Press

Font:
Bookman Old Style

Front cover photograph by:
Dave Lewis

For Eve

Special thanks to John Evans for his continued support and creative input.

Various poems have appeared previously in the following magazines or webzines: Read This Magazine, Square, Poetry Scotland, Bottom of the World, Tontine, Gloom Cupboard, Bolts of Silk, The beat, Treeblog, Spark Bright, New Magazine & Origami Condom.

CONTENTS

Sunday	pp 9
41 Ladysmith Road	pp 10
Your colour was love	pp 11
Stevie Nicks	pp 12
Africa	pp 13
A chance encounter	pp 14
Lightfoot	pp 15
Morning Sue	pp 16
October Sighting	pp 17
Hope	pp 18
Monday, after a phone call	pp 19
Kenya	pp 20
Grinding Down	pp 21
I Love a Wednesday	pp 23
With A Yes And A No	pp 24
Portrait of Churchill	pp 26
Boats	pp 27
Welsh Steam Train	pp 28
The Poppy Field	pp 29
A Kenyan Accident	pp 30
Y Bont	pp 31
Miners Dog	pp 32
Pen-Y-Fan	pp 33
Glass Monsters	pp 34
Gdansk Shipyards, 2006	pp 35
Wordsworth in 2006	pp 36
Layer Cake	pp 37
Kris Cross	pp 38

the Past in Colour   pp 39

Easter Baby   pp 40

UTI2   pp 41

Diagnosis   pp 42

Lung Shadow   pp 43

Helpless Chair   pp 44

Eve's First Travels   pp 45

Over Weekend Washed Cobbles   pp 46

Café Poets   pp 47

Dragonfly   pp 48

Afternoon Shift   pp 49

Fear   pp 50

Tenerife Club Singer   pp 52

Skips a Beat   pp 53

Valleys Haiku   pp 55

Human Nature   pp 58

Glazed Olives   pp 59

Whale's Tails   pp 60

Season's End   pp 61

Local Bus   pp 62

Shallow   pp 63

Fragment   pp 65

Toothless   pp 66

Sunday

With your hands that once held mine you turn the
    tired pages.
You're wearing boots and jeans, but best you're
    wearing flowers.
I've never been so unhappy in my life.

Searching smiles and seven thighs,
No luck, just more adventure,
The wind still blows,
The drink still flows,
My eyes still roll
Around the goldfish bowl...

Chocolate on a Thursday,
Cheese and tomato too,
Pictures on a Wednesday,
Ducks feeding me and you.

Sundays always fuck me up.

41 Ladysmith Road

I cuddle your mind like a duvet
Your pixie ears
  like Tiny Tim

You wear a green velvet hat
To move your possessions
  and my seed

Floating home
I hold my head high
  like a skyscraper

You colour was love

Sometimes on a winters day
When the sun has run away
I take out your song and photograph
That used to make me laugh.

Your smile so sweet
Your lips like fruit
Your eyes so bright - alive.

Oh you know sometimes...
Oh sometimes I just love you
I love you so much, I feel warm inside
And all my dreams
For just a minute they all disappear.

The leaves are falling near the old church
I think of you with me
Kicking, kicking
Gold before our eyes.

Your skin so smooth
Your wardrobe full of flowers
Your love so pure and strong - alive.

I wish you were with me
I wish I could remember
The colour of your love
'cos your colour was all over me
You coloured me.
Your colour was love.

Stevie Nicks

With Dylan, Blake and Shakespeare
It was warm

A gothic storm so smooth
It was fine

Your red lips and black records
It was good

Wine bottles full of candles
It was there

Stormy mattress soft
It was happy

Hey, I was just passing
And love was never mentioned

Africa

We were all cold
Now we're warm,
You taste of beer
And need to brush your hair -
Tell me something nice.

The kiss of morning dew
Pitter-patters on your eyes,
Night creatures go to sleep
As the daylight appears -
Tell me something nice.

How long can you hold out
In the country of our children?
The rains will come
And the rains will pass -
Tell me something nice.

One day in the distance
We'll be free and happy
The trees will grow, the sun will shine,
And you will smile and love me when -
I tell you something nice.

A chance encounter

A chance encounter 'neath the children's books
Shot me back to Autumn's past.
My stomach tight, my lips all dry,
Your hair and smile and smell so good.

Lightfoot

Fire, fresh
Green eyes, gold hair
Tastes of basketball

Flushed bright,
Fast, fight
Push, shove
Grab
Love

A sweat red smile
All golden
Home, hot
Start, stop
Stop, start
Touching night with prayer

Feed ducks
Again
A poem,
Kept
Kiss.

Morning Sue

Oh listen rain to the sound of her breathing,
Don't tap so loud you might wake her.
In the haze of this morning
She's a shape like heaven.

Don't shine so bright you might blind her,
Oh look at what you've done!
She stirs and turns her head,
Her hair is honey, sticky on my face.

I wonder what wonders she's making?
How much she is giving.
Who is she caring for?
Only the flowers know.

And as I slip back to the safety of my pillow,
She tells the rain to be quiet,
She scold's the sun for burning me,
She kisses my eyes to taste my dreams,
To see all my suffering.

And she wonders what wonders go to make a
    morning.
As the rain stops we hear the motorway.
Guess he was too kind,
It rained all night, to protect us...
From the waiting day.

October Sighting

The sky was the colour of the road,
Your hair was like autumn scenes,
The sun crept through and made your smile all
  golden.

And your face becomes mine,
Your eyes shine bright,
The memories return like light after night,
Creeping, your longings excite you,
I'm smiling at mirrors -
All of our shape and form.

Hope

I went to the forest to see what I could find.
I found a creature in the trees, writing songs upon
   the leaves.
And his words were oh so true
And his words were oh so kind.

He told stories of Man's wars, he told stories of
   Man's greed,
But no one heard his lyrics, no one heard his cries.
The grown-ups wouldn't listen and they told the
   children lies.
And all the time the forest was dying seed by seed.

Now the wind has blown like wintertime
And they've chopped the forest down.
The warnings and the prophecies, they're lost and
   dead and gone.
Except for this one precious leaf shouting its
   Autumn song.

Monday, after a phone call

The time for our coupling was set,
Our eyes and our hormones had met.
I was rushing my dinner,
Racing through sleep,
Wishing my days away.
To be one step closer,
One hour nearer,
I was worshipping the route I'd take.
Tasting the love we'd make.

Kenya

Who made the earth all red?
Was it the blazing sun
Or the blood of ten thousand dead?

Let me take you into me.
Let me inhale your sweetness.
I crave the peace you offer,
I've been looking and now I see.

Can I capture your total patience?
And hold you deep and long within me.
To merge, combine and fix.
This is my poetical deliverance.

For you made the earth so red,
And you rained through the blazing sun.
You shot rainbows through my dreams,
My heart and soul.
The rescue is in progress.

Grinding Down

Savage, night-masked demon befriends you
as the fevered rambling mind is unleashed,
feel the warm breeze on the street named freedom –
Thomas Mboya lived here once.
There's a smell of hot cakes and burnt coffee
at the stroke of a drunken 4am.
Will the ghosts of the liberators protect us?
Will they see all the muggers and shamens
that bewitch and entice you to sleep?
chapati's so safe they surround you
with the warmth of the company chef
where there's always some room for large talk
of revolution from any colour but mine
I'm not as strong as the tea, see,
maybe I'm a government spy?
Do you sober as quick?
in a morning too quickly for reason
and a parasite has long since tucked in
to your naked, writhing body –
teenaged and lonesome
with all your lovers overseas.
Teeming your hormones arouse lust
suppressed by sweet drugs and long absence
but black magic is sex and its blood
it will awaken the primitive man.
Meanwhile whilst electioneering
in fall it's the genocide season
with religion no cure
for pencil-less writers
for soul-starved musicians and jailbirds.
A continent smothered in damp forests
and deserts and bushland and plains
chiefs, rulers and kings
presidents for life
mortals are just run of the mill –
heart stew anyone?
Meanwhile I'm thinking, surviving the night club,
preparing the taxi-haggle banter
the misty in-betweens and singer of songs

carefully sucking air
guarding from self-mutilation –
we are returned to the hot summer night
when Nairobi is stirring, shaking and dancing
(unlike Carnivores acceptably modern)
you eat zebra and crocodile too
but giraffe is not nearly so popular.
'neath the city's choking haze,
the homeless lost night
is searching for savage embrace
to regain the passion, ignite the dark past
that history books wrongly accuse.
How can you judge me?
uninspired and forgotten
by friends and by family alike
there's a broken heart at the top of the kopje
it has my name on, added to the list
like a cup winners trophy, a memorial stone
twisting and laughing in space
through my fevered rambling's
my honour is gone
the collapse is as complete as your face.

I Love a Wednesday

What happens to a daydream?
Does it hide away when someone speaks?
Turn into driftwood on the stream
Or dig its claws in flesh
And watch the bloody bacon streak.

When you're happy with your life you never
    daydream.
When you're busy all the while you get no time.
When you lose the dreamless days that's just fine,
But sometimes you get a break, a chance to wonder,
And your world comes crashing down like rain with
    thunder.

With a Yes and a No

She can take you out
With her hand and a look
And a smile and a word
A few words, a few words,
Just a few more words,
And if you really want, if you really want,
You can take her up with a yes and a no,
With a yes and a no,
And with a yes and a no
She can do anything,
Anywhere, somehow,
With those fingers that grip,
All around, all around,
They're holding you tight,
Until the feelings gone,
Holding your mind
And all your thoughts and deeds,
With a yes and a no.

And you can take her beyond
The lips and the touch
Of her mouth so warm,
With her feelings inside,
You can take her out,
With a brush of your tongue,

And the words come too,

And the hand holds tight,

Like a drowning man,

You struggle and fight,

To let her out,

With a yes or a no,

With a yes and a no,

With a yes and a no.

Portrait of Churchill

Brooding pug faced tunic –
As heavy as a Lancaster.
Strong as a bull.
He sits thin lipped, silent and pale.
As drawn as a battle –
Heavy papers hem him in.

Boats

Boats

Water waiting

Sticky stranded seals

Cold as frozen rope

As abandoned as the night

Netted masts under skull shell sky

Breathless blood, salty seagull mud

Beached boats, beached boats

Sardine stained wood

Hollow hope

Boats

Welsh Steam Train

Whistles stir the beast –
Steamy dawns the dinosaur
Metal monster warmed

...Winter breath
Cold dawn, steam smoke
Working, braking, stopped

Black light
Sleepy tracks
Shadows waking up

The Poppy Field

A sunset
Swaying in summer –
Crowded green grass

Purple pink...
 Poppies red
Fields of yellow light

Stretching flat and filtered
 Away –
The distant trees are black

A Kenyan Accident

Flamingo's fly where she goes
The jeep wheel spinning free
Blue, blue orange sky
Nakuru's baked white pink.

She once was loving, laughing
Watched children – shout, sing, smile.
Red fast, brown hot, too fast, too fast
Then she's crashing craters.

Sweet sweat that tastes of rock
Killing, killing
Tilt, untracked –
The acacia standing guard.

Now creamy skin all torn
Blood eyes that
Stare at lava
Children's faces frozen time.

Y Bont

Old miners lamp surveys the scene
Of Nationalist flags hung high as martyrs
The silent piano waits.

There's plaster scars, the clip clop of shoes
Leather from long dead horses.

Dragon chases dragon
Above the factory lights
Of Carling, Bow and Stella
Pumped tight, pulled long
  Delicate, slow,
Like absent lovers do.

Humid cotton armpits
The bar blonde smells of possession
While wobbled voices shadow.

Suits one and two and three
Shout bald after a funeral.
Wet sheepdog smells –
No perfume on a Monday.
The air - a smokers kiss
Of woodworm breath.

Miner's Dog

High home summer hill
Straining, sucking, sitting
Staring, stopped and stick-
A pit-prop tight and gripped.

The trees across the valley
Much higher than he can go now.
I pant to reassure him
In time with his withered eyes.

His tongue, tombed gritty green
He's faithful, though he's fading
Bones in death-grey jumper
Where will he lead me next?

Pen-Y-Fan

The green blades slice calf skin. Shred.
Bloodlines soft, don't hurt.
Stomping through birdsong –
Sweet and shouting.

Orange cheeks blushed loud,
Shadows can't sleep in motion.
Shells crunched.
Solid air.

Deep blue merges into pale blue lightning fast.
Ripping sails of ozone, cream daubed, canvas green.
"Baaaaaaaaaaaa"
Muttering sun, alone on earth parched tongue.

Noisy water whistling.
I'm sitting, breathing freedom.
Gulping.
The silence too loud to dream.

Glass Monsters

Looking at the statue of Archibald Hood in Llwynypia

Slate peeling, paint stripped
Bricks through glass monsters
Making top hats, rabbits, seahorses.

Statue standing regal
Above a sea of weeds and grass.

Coal owner clean – valley grey
Mr Hood showing the way... away.

Gdansk Shipyards, 2006

Vultures leaning. Thin with age. Massive metal. Oil.
Idle as the breeze that stills the cool canal.

A rat drags a dead pigeon underwater. The grey,
green film ripples to the bang, bang, bang of
   hammers.

The docker's bars are empty, tram-stops silent as
   graves.
Now miserably beautiful women wear amber on
   perfect skin.
Hiding hardships.

Welders golden fire lights up old hunchbacked men.
As they stand. Hot-coated. Shoulder to shoulder
Like good luck symbols.
Silent soldiers.
Guarding the stark, fragile future.

Wordsworth in 2006

Away from the public path
he turned his usual steps
and hitched a ride with me.

We spoke of metal machines
and plastic things that
etched his stony brow.

We sailed in silence, sweet
past mountains, streams and rocks
shaped like a scream.

Crows bickered overhead
as the road stretched out
Wordsworth looked out the window.

Puzzled.

Layer Cake

Framed family snapshots – like peas in a pod
Box one full of children – happy as toys
Terrace upon terrace, row upon row.

Life like life, lives like lives
Breathing, loving happy cages
The future as dead as grannies bed.

Box two still belonging – no strangers here
Miners, sisters, lovers, dogs and open doors –
Like layer cake cuddling rainbows.

Kris cross

, sky blue Kris cross
, Jenna Jameson curls
, mini-bonbons
, jellyfish tits
, tanned plump-pins
, herhat glued on
, hairsprayed –
, stuck with sumit' anyhow...
, while riding the valley's
, mmm...
meanwhile in another part of town her best friend
and bisexual lover has a six shooter aimed at your
crotch...
and
there's lilac smocks and nurses uniforms in our
21st Century town
it's a beautiful wigarama sunset
with masala-blood stained tiles
  and
    shabby ceilings,
      rotting roof and pissy glass,
pigeoned shit
  and feathered former
  local porn stars that didn't make it big
(reduced to begging online)
and
dog-wet cardboard,
vibrators spanking concrete
until their batteries flop
flop-lap, drunk-dance
too cheap and lonely to be sleazy,
the plastic-bag perfume
, harbours dreams
, o

the Past in Colour

we   are   just   a

       speck   a   sparrow's

     heartbeat,   yellow-lonely

        leaves,   clinging on,   thru'

creeping   cold,   distilling   dust

       branching   shadows

         hiding   grains of

sand   the   hollow   storm

blast   comes   painted

     insect   wings   waiting for

       the crush

the   muffled   crunch

Easter Baby

You were an Easter baby
We might have called you Brecon.
Cocooned in tubes, like snakes
  in the Garden of Eden.

"She's got attitude that one!"
Pulling out her lines,
Eager to live,
Seven weeks
  keener than nature.
And a miniature grip
Strong as a lion.

UTI 2

From bed to chair
Love runs to care
Eyes shut, skin white
Her body slight

She once saved my life
With black and white smiles
Her love it grew
My insides renewed

Now helpless me
Looks on in fright
I want to give
Please take all of me

Diagnosis

It was the 17th of June, a Friday.
A day when the sun came out and dried up all the
   rain.
A day like any other day.

But today was different
Today they told my dad he'd get treatment.
He sighed, seemed indifferent.

Mam held my hand,
Like she did when Uncle Alf died.
Oblivious of horrors they didn't understand.

God you cunt – you just don't care
Is this all we have to look forward to?
It's not fucking fair.

Lung Shadow

Oh glorious birth with spring defending
How wondrous life so young,
When days were warm and never-ending.
There were no shadows on your lung.

Careless smoke and summer wheezes
And all too soon you'd loved and lost.
Broken bones and caught diseases,
Saved all your pennies at all costs.

The vibrant world stands still
As strong men shed a stone a week
They fade and stare at autumn's will.
Death coughs - plays hide and seek.

The helpless watchers make not a dent
I guess all our lives are waste.
When winter reeks of disappointment.
And all we ever knew is time encased.

Helpless Chair

Your body still now and you're peaceful.
Since yesterday we're very breath aware.
With pale blue linen all around you,
We're understanding what it is to care.

The night is silent, save for you.
Your lungs have travelled many roads.
While drugs are pumped and driven veinwards,
Your pillows' heavy with their load.

I guess now is not the end of time,
Although the leaves are turning brown.
We all think winters' when it snows
But cold can come without a sound.

Eve's First Travels

One blue steel morning
Your rainbow eyes
Captured my immortality

Crushing footballs of dew drops
With your magic adventure
My lips touched impatient fire

Then the antique sun
All snake scaled dry
Faded when she went away

Now, we're following the old path
Of moonlit bat shadows
And the reed jailed river

Ripples on
Ripples on
Ripples on

Your eyelids flicker
Dream-captured memories
Laughter, now Daddy's gone.

Over Weekend Washed Cobbles

Over weekend washed cobbles
Dawn damp beer brown
Coughing men trudge
Back to hell

Oblivious to the velvet hills
Where flowers salsa and sing
The cough gets worse
Through sugar-lonely tea

Now time has seen enough
Injects sunshine - brief like heroin
To cut diamond sharp
And wash away pebbled-dashed bones

While Mammy's shoes
Tap-dance on and on
'till photographs rot
Out of children's memories

Café poets...

Café poets...
    they sit in coffeehouses in Pontcanna
    talking to the media types
    about their next holiday
    they call it a bursary
    a journey of discovery
    "I got the grant you see,
    I've always wanted to go...
    ...to South America"

Café poets...
    so hard done by
    such sacrifices they make
    de-caffed and tea-stained
    their livers and souls
    full of corporate tuna
    free range and feta'd
    to the Middle East
    they'll never really see

Café poets...
    it'll be Africa next
    when Babylon and Mongolia
    are out of season
    like cabbages or rape seed
    think about it
    shout about it
    and be damned
    ha, ha

Café poets...
    once coal-mined and iron-ored
    now just whore
    charging for appearance
    charge for lectures
    charge for bullshit
    packaged from their new house
    "...it's on my laptop, honey!"
    "I have a dinner party responsibility"

Dragonfly

One bone cold afternoon
   when love had died a thousand years before
   a dragonfly did land,
upon my wrinkled hand
   and in glossy green and yellow
     and composite matt black
the veins of life
   the fragile mesh
     forced my heart to see
       and
liked me.

Afternoon Shift

The lino shiny dead
  cramped crocodile
choked hand
  bread and dripping
at the cupboard towers
  arthritic apron
dogs at feet
  her petal splits
cuts like crusts
  she knows you know
sliced chestnut
  men at work
the knock on wood
  saltwater drips on fur

Fear

what I really want to say is FUCK!
but that would be uncouth and uncalled for
so I secrete in my fragile shell
of responsibility
and fear
of loneliness
of being outcast
from reels
from wheels
and teams
of TV and radio stars
magazine gloss
and fatty
whispered lips as I pass
shunned by statues
at bus stops
or trains
in the street
while their motion
never-ending
factory-like death march
towards white noise
and stupor
unstoppable
not possible
impassable
in this kingdom
of mobile wii wee wee
and howling now
as innocence
is brushed from my genome
too quickly
like earthquakes
to die
is my nightmare
without living
without breathing
without feeling
without love

I hate it
my veil-cage
tyre-tight
and the wall
on my chest
too heavy
too late
to stop

Tenerife Club Singer

Alone at the bar
Two packs of cigarettes
Are stacked like long lost friends
The club singer sits alone

Constant in his loneliness
As transit tourists chat
For two weeks at a time
His world, their world, complete

Alone he sits and smokes
Smokes himself to death
Only home for the NHS
Bald 'neath his cowboy hat

Skips a Beat

the city lights are shining

through a sky that's brilliant blue

freaks and fags and fall-downs

look like Doris Day

the feeling is surprising

my heart it...

skips a beat

walking in the footsteps

howling at the ghosts

I'm thinking of my mother

and I'm not 46...

yet

drinking at Vesuvio's

add Dylan to my Laugharne

topping up my Kinski

Hendrix castles - Muslim sand

the feeling is enlightening

but my heart it...

skips a beat

so until we see the ocean

when it fades back to

now-time

this feeling is my feeling

how can we capture moments?

when there's nothing permanent

and everyone from Elvis

to Jesus

skips a beat

Valleys Haiku

That wet flavour
Obese moon
Spewing tides

Over cobbles
While November
Looks on lost

In Asda
Shiny plastics
dull short memory

Llanwonno jungle
Steals the stolen
Torched cars

Rust never sleeps
Eats the autumnal
Factory gate

Rugby poets mew
They voice cathedral
of blended hope

In dead man's pool
Their diesel killed our newts
For the A470

I fuck and fly
With abandoned buttons
sucking snowdrops

Your face a film
That dances fire
thru' winter's whisky

Ruby chocolate
glowing dusks
through silent branches

Demons flutter up
No bluebell harvest
To corrupt the dead

In my time of breathing...
Pint glasses gashing
'neath bellies bright

Supping sixth form
Bragg, Cole, The Jam
"That's Entertainment"

Muffled moon
Big Sur sunrise
Just an ancient dream now

Tramp refuses bed for the night
Must be hardly
Winter

No strawberries
No starlight, no golden
Precinct petals

"What's a pit da?"
Acne scarred mountains
Earthquake baggage

Bougainvillea hangs
Inside a plastic bag
Logo   suffocates

While café poets
Leak middle class piss
Over property dreams

Towers sketched
Upon the star black
Cold walk home

Credit crunched
Startled bunnies
Tunes change

In bistro mosques
ISA chat
Radiator shimmer

Hamster eyes
Bead inconsequential
Ambulance in street

Half Moon
bulldozer
New dawn curried

Ashes of children
Make it slightly tricky
To talk of patches

Full circle
Drawn with a needle
Frozen eyes

Full on
Our passionate lives
Need a new moon

Human Nature

"Hey man!"
grated the Californian
"You left your *Howl* behind"
"Wow!"
"Did you hear that?" said Paulie

"Only in this city man,
    and leave it to me,
        I'll get the man to sign it yeh,
            and if you don't hear from me
                let me know and ask
                    me to send the fuckin' book"

I left my friend a note.
My best friend in half an hour.

"Send me the fuckin' book man!"
I wrote.
He laughed.

Now I wait in the rain in a land devoid
of oranges
for the postman.

Glazed Olives

your granddaddy whipped black men
with rubber hoses across their feet
extracting state secrets
to keep his baby safe
upon the rainbow street

now your apple-green eyes
interrogate me in this new town
where we replace petrol-soaked throats
with meanwhiles and maybes
and your soft eiderdown

Whale Tails

I   met   a   tangerine   who   was
    far far far from   home.   And in
        a   downtown   Durban
;   bar we swapped t-shirts,
; ;   ;   smiles   and   ;
;   beer. Your
           flow ing
           hair was
;;   loose as
           we spoke
        of sharks
        and whales.
        "; ; " ", ; ;

      (((ripples – ripples – ripples)))

  (((ripples – ripples – ripples – ripples)))

(((ripples – ripples – ripples –ripples – ripples)))

(((ripples – ripples –ripples – ripples – ripples)))

      who knows

    what's beneath

      the surface eh?

Season's End

I smile soft and pretend to assimilate,
I absorb the "Hya butt's" and laughing eyes,
Sip ale, gulp wine
And make them think I think
So much of them
Only pulling off sincerity
When I see
Coming over to me
A copper cockroach flashing
Scuttling for my crumbs
And stops my soul
From rotting
Christmas time.

Local Bus

hya but
'ow are you 'n
I've got three blocks in my arteries see
but they won't operate 'cos of my age
how old are you then?
I'm ninety see mun
it's my legs
and my missus is on about her birthday party
I told her don't be so soft
she's bloody ninety too next Spring
I used to drink heavy like
and smoke
but she put paid to that see
aye, can't walk too far now see
bloody bus is always late an' all
hmm,
sa' right
aye

Shallow

"Hey, did you happen to see the most beautiful girl in the world?"
her name is Candy
she's quite handy
with shots and ecstasy
a regular designer-dance-debutante

        Meanwhile, plain Jane is getting signatures
                to stop them cutting
                out brains of bunnies
              she can't sleep for hearing
                cries of puppies

"Wow, what a dress, scarf and hat!"
I have to have them
to **party**, *party*, ***party***
"No time for work mun!"
this summer's so hot

           The sky is bruising nicely now...
        there's lead at the end of her rainbow
              she misses Bob Dylan
              EBay'd Wilfred Owen
        to renew her dolphin membership

But no sweaty thighs or magic eyes
will stop her in her tracks
the Chelsea Hotel **FOR SALE?**
her nose rots in the garden of plenty
and time leapfrogs to now...

           And she's still sewing silks
        for babies bedroom bedspread
      an eco-traveller with Marrakech mint tea
    reading about Van Gogh and William Burroughs
                smelling rain

Depression when they meet again
"How long has it been? Where did it go?"
since I drank the ocean
since you wore rags and beads
and talked in Spanish

But, I'm just beginning?
"Don't you see it?"
how deep and blue and never-ending...
my feelings are foundations
to fly me to the moon

Fragment

beneath a bowl of concrete coloured sky
wildfire hair and lion's eyes
stab diamonds through my heart

but how come she evolves?
how come she sees more?
how come she's so fragile?
when I ask for more?

and when I reach the bottom
when I can't go on no more
when life's air-con overwhelms me
when it penetrates my bones

she's there when she's needed
to pick me up again
she's hiding in a tiny corner of my mind

Toothless

1.

thigh

petals of
perfume

petals of
violence

the
jagged
map

the familiar
space

2.

shallow

valley

cleaves

neap-tide

frothy

3.

red and pink
through repetition

you can just feel
my fingers smiling

adding, subtracting
ever after

and it takes twenty years
to reciprocate

the blossom of
mustard seed